Nudes of 16 Lands

Nudes of 16 Lands

by Stewart Rothman

AMPHOTO

American Photographic Book Publishing Co., Inc.

NEW YORK

This book is dedicated to the women in my life—
Leslie, Karen, and Lee.

Published in New York by American Photographic Book Publishing Co., Inc.

Library of Congress Catalog Card Number 67-18637.

Manufactured in the United States of America.

Foreword

Stewart Rothman walked into my office one day and offered me a moose steak. I am accustomed to potential authors making rash promises, but I had never been offered moose before, so I felt that this man deserved, at the least, to be heard out. He justified the hearing. It is too coy, perhaps, to describe him as an "Alaskan kodiak bear," but he *is* big and bearded, bluff and hearty, and the free-and-easy spirit that characterizes any frontier region is in him. In fact, it is him. Stu stayed in Alaska after a wartime hitch; he hunts (yes, moose, and caribou and deer) and fishes and generally enjoys being an Alaskan. He is also a very fine photographer.

A while back he gathered together his family and hied them off to Europe. There, he realized a long-held dream: to bring together his love for figure photography with the scenic and ethnic wonders of new lands. This book is the result of that synthesis. There was no shortage of excellent pictures to choose from; on the contrary, Stu came to New York with three suitcases full. And those were just proofs. He and I spent many hours poring over contact sheets, and in that time I learned a great deal about the man and his work.

Stewart Rothman has fused his personality with his profession—he has managed to yoke exuberant enthusiasm to exacting technique and produce work that is both vital and fine, earthy yet well-wrought. He does not take "classical" nudes nor, except for his salon pictures, does he hew to the rules for form and lighting. He does not even nod to the conventions of outdoor figure work—making the girl look like a rock and the rock a girl. Instead, Stu brings to these photographs a comprehension of the whole—girl plus country plus time—and his own deep appreciation of and love for woman, to create a new genre of nude altogether. His French model is all that Frenchwomen are or have been in the loving mind's eye: his Spanish woman is soft and tawny and real; his Greek girl is Greece—strong, angular, and still delicate. For Stewart does not make of nude photography a cool, academic exercise. He knows and feels.

This collection of nudes, then, is not ordinary. It is infused with a single man's spirit, shining in the lands he came to know, reflected from the flesh he understands. It is a rare mixture.

JOHN C. WOLF
Editor-in-Chief
AMPHOTO

Contents

Author and model in the Isabell Pass; 1/125 sec. at *f*/11 500EL, with 30-foot remote release, 150mm lens.

Alaska

It appeared to be a great idea—the culmination of a dream I had nourished as far back as 1948, when I was a photographer stationed in General MacArthur's headquarters in Tokyo, Japan. As a free lance photographer in Alaska for 11 years, I had let my dream grow to glacier proportions. Someday I would pack up my wife and children, hire a governess in England, and tour Europe. In each country I would select a woman who seemed to me to epitomize her nationality, and I would photograph her artistically in her native habitat and in the nude.

All I had ever needed, or so I thought, was money with which to finance the trip. And now, by a stroke of good fortune, I had the money. The rest would be simple. I would "borrow" the money from myself and repay it by selling stock pictures of foreign scenic views, industries, and people at work and play. Not until I felt I had enough saleable stock photos to repay my expenses in a country would I permit myself a busman's holiday and photograph nudes.

I still think the idea was fundamentally sound, but inexperience began to throw me off course from the very start. For one thing, I didn't always have credentials that people in different foreign countries could read or interpret accurately. Another mistake was in not taking along sample prints of nudes I'd photographed in Alaska and New England. Without samples to judge, many people were skeptical of my artistic ability or sincerity.

My third and greatest mistake, perhaps, was that of seeking the professional advice of editors and picture buyers in the United States and then forgetting what they had told me each time I focused upon a nude in a new locale. This forgetfulness may have been subconsciously deliberate. The editors and buyers were thinking in terms of saleable pictures—the pseudo-sexy nudes you see in so many books, magazines, and barber shop calendars. I wasn't. In photographing the nude, I have never bothered with the so-called "rules" of camera technique, much less with either public or commercial appetites in pictures. It is neither the model, the public, nor my photographic peers that I am out to please. I feel that the expenditure of my films, camera equipment, travel expenses, model fees, and time entitles me to the self-indulgence of pleasing myself first. If this be provincial or in any other way reproachable—so be it!

In shooting for my own satisfaction, however, I have always observed certain rigid, self-imposed policies. I do not photograph a nude without a chaperon present. In posing a subject, I subscribe to voice direction; under no circumstances do I touch a model in order to achieve a head, hand, or body posture. I make it a point not to permit a model to wear earrings, bracelets, beads, or any other type of jewelry or costume. To my mind, these "personalize" a subject, as does a smile or direct "looking into the camera" gaze. In brief, I'm not interested in the sexy, challenging, or provocative interpretations of the nude.

While serving with the armed forces in Japan and Korea, I had access to all types of camera and darkroom equipment. By the time I was ready to set up my own studio in Alaska, I had begun to favor single-lens reflex cameras with interchangeable lenses and film magazines. At times, I used a studio camera (Linhof) on a tripod—even outdoors while I wore a heavy parka and my model wore gooseflesh. In the darkroom where critics say I excel, I splurged for everything from the best enlarger and processing equipment I could find to supplies of 16″ x 20″ salon-type printing papers that set me back a small fortune. All of this was literally wiped out by the recent earthquake and floods, which converted Fairbanks into an instant disaster area.

Model relaxes at two degrees above freezing. (The chaperon was standing by with a large blanket, which she used to cover the model for ten minutes after every five minutes of shooting.) 1/125 sec. at *f*/11, Hasselblad 500C, 150mm lens.

The model was photographed through a brandy glass filled with water and ½ inch of cooking oil on the top, with a wick burning as a candle. I brought out these interesting reflections by focusing neither on the model or the glass but on the model's image in the water. All lighting was directed at the model; no light except the spill light was allowed to strike the glass; 1/30 sec. at *f*/8, Hasselblad 500C, 80mm lens.

A low key semi-silhouette illuminated by one overhead floodlight; 1/30 sec. at *f*/5.6, Hasselblad 500C, 80mm lens.

I was virtually uninsured and could salvage almost nothing from my flood-silted studio. Had the pictures you see here not been thousands of miles away with my agent at the time of the flood, there would have been no record of my overseas trip and no book.

Now, as I recoup my losses, I find that I am reducing my taste in equipment to strict essentials. The 2¼" x 2¼" single-lens reflex, magazine back cameras are still my first choices. I stick with a few interchangeable lenses ranging from wide-angle to 500mm telephoto. As always, each lens has a UV 15 filter that remains on it at all times. Although this filter doesn't affect exposure, it protects the relatively soft surfaces of the optical glass from sand, snow, and salt spray. If the overseas trip taught me to prepare in advance, the Fairbanks' disaster taught me something equally important, that is, restrict your equipment to what you will actually use and insure it!

I think that the question other shutterbugs ask me most frequently goes something like this, "How come you can get nonprofessional models to pose in the nude for you so easily?"

Who says I get them "easily"? In some parts of Europe, just as in some parts of North America, it took days to decide on the type of model I wanted and still more time to find a woman who was willing to pose in the nude. In some parts of the world, my best efforts were like so many sales pitches spoken into the wind. I simply couldn't find a model I wanted to photograph.

As a rule, however, my batting average in finding models is high. I think this is partially because I make no bones about the fact that I am looking for a certain type of woman to pose in the nude for art studies. If possible, I show samples and credentials. I spread the word around openly and without apology or embarrassment. If I see a woman I think might fill the bill, I convey my interest point-blank—preferably, through a formal introduction but, if necessary, via my card accompanied by a request to speak to her.

Many women thus approached turn thumbs down on the idea, but rarely, if ever, is a woman miffed when tactfully asked. After all, there is a compliment implied when she has been singled out from other women because one artist considers her more strikingly or interestingly endowed than other women. Some of the most gracious women I have ever met have thanked me profusely for the honor, while turning me down.

Any door-to-door salesman, however, can tell you the secret of getting sales—or models—in volume. It lies in ringing enough doorbells, or asking enough women to pose. The law of averages guarantees the rest.

A study in form; 1/30 sec. at *f*/8, Hasselblad 500C, 80mm lens. Note: The shadow on the background was formed by one of the floodlights shining through a bamboo chair.

Again, the model through a brandy glass. Here too, it was her reflected image I focused on.

The world is full of models, women who are willing to pose from vanity, for money, or a combination of both, if they are convinced that the photographer's motives are what he claims. It is up to the individual photographer to provide proof positive that his motives and the uses to which the resulting pictures will be put are agreeable to everyone concerned.

Women are not naïve. If you aren't honest in your intentions, forget nude photography. Even the most dimwitted potential model will soon see through a phony as clearly as if he were made of crystal glass. But if you are on the level, my advice is don't hem or haw. Have respect for your work, conviction in its propriety, and guts enough to ask the best subject you find to pose in the nude. The worst she can do is decline, and if you are as sincere as you should be, she will probably decline regretfully.

Since I use professional models as rarely as possible, most of my subjects have never posed before in the nude. They are technically amateurs—secretaries, working girls, and housewives. I steer away from girls whom I know to be professional pin-up or nude models, and I never impose upon my models' privacy by inquiring into their personal lives or backgrounds.

This doesn't prevent my playing a guessing game long after a shooting session is over. I once discovered that a model I had photographed was a relative of the local police commissioner. Another was a school teacher. Still another demure miss proved to be a gyrating "go-go" girl after dusk.

I think the one I'll always remember was the sweet-faced miss I met and photographed in one of the countries represented in the pages that follow. She was introduced to me by a devout churchgoer, who spoke enthusiastically about the way she held his youngsters enthralled as a Sunday school teacher. Throughout the entire session I saw her gentle, almost angelic personality shining through in nearly every pose. When we returned to her village in mid-afternoon, the kids swarmed about her like bees, begging for Bible stories. I had difficulty getting close enough to pay her for posing, and whatever she said to me in farewell was lost in the din of the children's chatter. I caught sight of the faces of villagers smiling as they watched her sit down beside the fountain in the town square and begin a story.

It was a month later when I learned by accident that she was known for 20 leagues in every direction as the "Queen" of a legion of girls for hire. When I think of her now as I view the pictures I shot, her personal life seems irrelevant. To me, she's the "Queen" of a totally different realm.

Germany

I felt uneasy as I stared at the Bradenburger Tor and the obscene wall that separates West Berlin from East Berlin. Even as I tried to absorb the shock of the scene before my eyes, workers on the other side were adding refinements that would make it even more difficult to escape their Communistic "Utopia."

Berlin wasn't even on my itinerary when I planned my trip to West Germany in search of a *fraulein* typical of this war torn and divided country. However, I just couldn't visit Germany and not see "the Wall." I'd read about it; I had even seen movies of East Germans being killed as they tried to escape over it, under it, and through it. Still, one cannot experience the full horror of this man-made physical and psychological barrier until he has seen it with his own eyes.

I gave an involuntary shudder as I turned away. This was no place for me to shoot pictures of a nude. The hard-working and brave people of West Berlin certainly typify the indomitable spirit of West Germany, but I was looking for a softer, more human symbol. There was nothing soft or human about "the Wall."

As my airliner took off and I looked down, it was evident that, despite the almost miraculous rebuilding of West Berlin, many scars of World War II remain and will for years to come.

The airliner flew over East German territory without incident, and I couldn't help thinking of the thousands of life-saving flights over this same area during the Berlin blockade. The United States and Britain flew in more than 1.5 million tons of foodstuffs during those trying months in 1948 and 1949 at a cost of $170,000,000.

Scene along the Berlin Wall showing the desolation in East Berlin and the modern construction in West Berlin; 1/125 sec. at *f*/11, Hasselblad 500C, 80mm lens.

It was this Herculean feat that kept the West Berliners from knuckling under to the Communists.

The crazy-quilt land unfolded quickly as we headed for Hamburg, the city-state on the Elbe, which was once called the "gateway to the world" because of the tremendous volume of goods shipped through its huge port facilities.

As we circled Fuhlsbuttel airport and entered the landing pattern, I was amazed by the modern look of Hamburg and the modern buildings. A friendly fellow passenger, a native of the city, explained the new look.

"More than 50 per cent of the residences and 60 per cent of the port installations were destroyed by bombing raids during the war," he said matter-of-factly in almost perfect English. "That's why you see so many new buildings. Quite a few of the old ones survived, though damaged."

I looked at him with sympathy and embarrassment. It's difficult for me to talk about bombings and killings at any time and even more so when my companion is a former enemy. You can hardly say, "Sorry about that," and continue the conversation in a nonchalant way.

"How many people were killed in Hamburg during the air raids?" I asked.

"I don't really remember," he said, his round red face puckered in thought, "but I do recall reading that 50,000 were killed during a two-month period. Actually, Kiel got hit even harder, with two-thirds of the city being destroyed by bombs."

"It doesn't seem real; it's too hard to imagine," I muttered, a bit lamely.

"*Ja!* It was real," my companion replied, in a voice no longer matter-of-fact. There was hurt in his blue eyes and tone of voice.

Driving around Hamburg, I readily saw that the destruction was, indeed, real. Modern apartment buildings, homes in the residential areas, and gleaming new office buildings in the heart of the city were silent memorials to destruction during the war. The old city hall with its towering spire was one of the historic buildings not destroyed by bombs.

Not finding the *fraulein* I was looking for, I motored the 70 miles to Kiel to see if it, too, had been restored. It was along this northeast coast of flatlands, dotted with marshes, that I found the shooting location I liked. It was at Kiel—modern now but retaining the atmosphere of the pre-war years—that I found the *fraulein* I

This model proved very difficult to photograph. She had some experience posing for a magazine and tended to strike sexy poses. I had to keep telling her (through the chaperon because she did not speak English) that I was not interested in this type of photography. Finally, she began to ignore me and concentrate on her surroundings, and I was able to capture these poses; 1/125 sec. at *f*/8, Hasselblad 500C, 80mm lens.

The operahouse in East Berlin photographed through a bridge for an interesting pattern; 1/60 sec. at *f*/11, Hasselblad 500C, 80mm lens.

was seeking. Blonde, blue-eyed, with a swan's neck and a beautiful body, she seemed to me to be the "all-German girl."

In speaking with her, I learned that she had posed professionally. Overcoming my self-imposed rule against using girls who were experienced models, I asked her if she would pose. She agreed.

The marshland I had chosen for location was ideal for the pictures I had in mind. I wanted to use selective focus, placing the emphasis on the model.

I soon discovered I had made a mistake in breaking my own rule about professional models. The *fraulein* was the most difficult subject I had during my tour. It wasn't that she was lacking in talent. In fact, the opposite was true. The problem was that since she had posed so many times for pin-up pictures, she instinctively assumed poses as I started to shoot. Unfortunately, her poses were more appropriate for semi-nude calendar photos than for impersonal nude art.

One point was in our favor; it was early April, and we had no trouble with mosquitoes, flies, or bugs. It was just a bit cool, however, and my model developed a bad case of goose bumps from time to time, which held up the shooting session.

Everything finally worked out all right. When she discovered exactly what it was I wanted, she settled down to work and forgot about her previous posing. With a bright sun high in the sky, I managed to get a number of good pictures.

"*Auf wiedersehen,*" she murmured, as we shook hands after dining in Kiel later that day. It's a phrase with a fascinating ring to it, one that includes a sincere request to come back again. Perhaps some day I will.

(Top left) The same model in a candid shot; 1/125 sec. at *f*/11, 150mm lens.

(Top right) Here I used an 80mm lens, at 1/125 sec. at *f*/11.

(Bottom) Checkpoint Charlie, the access point to East Berlin; 20 sec. at *f*/8, Hasselblad 500C, 80mm lens.

The beach along the waterfront; 1/125 sec. at *f*/11, Hasselblad 500C, 80mm lens.

Monaco

If the principality of Monaco was a lump of wet clay in the hands of a giant, he could modify its shape and set it down in Central Park in New York. All 370 acres of Monaco would fit into the park with room to spare.

Although the French and Italian Riviera were bathed in fog the day I arrived, I soon discovered Monaco's chief reason for being. The manufacturing of beautiful postage stamps and the crowning of princesses are *not* the major industries. Affluent tourists swarm to Monte Carlo for the "sports." Some derive soulful satisfaction from observing small white cubes bounce over flat areas of green baize. Others are fascinated by the whirring, spinning, and clicking of big wheels. The only adults not permitted by law to gamble in the casinos are the natives of Monaco. For strangers who take no pleasure in casino sports, a variety of other pastimes have been thoughtfully provided by various managements. These include swimming, touring, fishing, boating, and partying.

Lady Luck did not favor me while I was in Monaco. The weather was overcast, the prices were inflated, and the women looked imported. Hunting for a nonprofessional figure model here was like hunting for an ice floe in the Sahara.

When I finally did manage to obtain a subject and arrange a shooting session on a rocky promontory off the Riviera coast, bad luck accompanied me. The wind was strong, the light was poor, and the shore rocks crawled with land crabs.

I had decided to use my Hasselblad camera with a 250mm lens and shoot wide open at 1/500 sec. That decision complicated

(Opposite) Sitting on a rock promontory jutting out into the Mediterranean; 1/125 sec. at *f*/11, Hasselblad 500C, 50mm lens.

Breakers cascading around the model as fishermen watch off shore; 1/500 sec. at *f*/5.6, Hasselblad 500C, 250mm lens.

the situation by placing distance between the camera and my subject. I could see that the combination of wind, sharp rocks, and land crabs was doing little to put my model in a relaxed mood for posing. I tried to reassure her, but the wind carried my voice away from her. When she finally reached the spot I had designated and began to calm down, I saw from the magnified telephoto image in the viewfinder that she was still wearing a necklace.

Since one of the things I insist upon in a nude study is total absence of jewelry, I shouted at her to remove the necklace. She couldn't hear me. I pantomimed taking it off. She complied. I shouted posing instructions. She still couldn't hear me. I acted them out myself and pointed at her. She complied.

Out on the water, a fisherman began to take an interest in our movements. Rowing leisurely, he approached the point of rocks and studied the model. Then he studied me with, I fancied, equal interest. He was too far away to hear what I said. That was probably fortunate for me. At length, he methodically turned his boat around and rowed away.

After he left, I exposed a few frames of film. But this simply wasn't my day. I motioned the model in, packed my gear, paid her posing fee, and headed for Monte Carlo. As soon as possible thereafter, I left Monaco to its tourist sports—and its damned land crabs.

Pigalle in Paris at night; 5 sec. at *f*/4, Hasselblad 500C, 80mm lens.

France

It's only natural to think of Paris first when looking for a model typical of France. Paris is probably a second home to more Americans than any other city in the world—at least to those Americans who do any traveling.

Just as any other average tourist, I was thrilled by this mammoth city with its ancient history, sidewalk cafés, booksellers' stalls along the River Seine, Notre Dame cathedral, the Arc de Triomphe on the west end of the Champs Elysées, the Eiffel Tower, and the many other landmarks and customs that give Paris its unique flavor. But, I decided, all of these were typical of Paris, not of France.

Still, I couldn't resist a visit to the Folies-Bergères to see *les girls*, rationalizing that I just might find one who would serve as my model. *Les girls* lived up to all of the advance publicity, but not one could be considered to be typical of France.

Hiring a motor car, I decided to drive down the coast to see more of the country and its people. Motoring through the Normandy area was a moving experience. Here the brave French bore the brunt of the hell and fury of the beginning of the end of the Third Reich. Here Allied forces scrambled ashore and clawed a foothold on the continent of Europe, one that would lead to the liberation of France. Yes, these people were certainly typical of the spirit of France, but I still couldn't find the girl to fill the role.

As I drove down the coast, headed for the famous Bordeaux area, I was certain that my French model, wherever I found her, would be living in an area of historic significance. What better region could I visit than Bordeaux, world famous seaport and home of some of the best wines in the world.

I found the Bordeaux wines every bit as fine as their reputation. They seemed even better than the Bordeaux wines I had enjoyed in the United States. If you haven't tried them, ask for a few of these: Château Lafite, or Château Haut-Brion, both red wines; and Château Yquem, a white wine.

I was impressed, too, by the enormity of this great port, some eight miles long, with its marshaling yards, wet docks, and network of railway yards. Wines are one of the most important items of trade to be shipped from this port. It is also a fishing port, with a large fleet making an annual pilgrimage to the fisheries off the coasts of Iceland and Newfoundland.

Bombed savagely by both the Germans and the Allied forces during World War II, Bordeaux was reoccupied by French patriots. Certainly, these sturdy folk were typical of the spirit of France.

But again, although I saw hundreds of beautiful girls with that enchanting, almost mystic attraction of French women, I wasn't satisfied that I had found the girl I was looking for.

I decided to cut across France and visit the Riviera, the playground of the idle rich from nations around the world. I didn't expect to find my model there, but was ready for a rest.

As I left Bordeaux I never dreamed I would come to a famous French city with a split personality—one that would provide me with both a typical background and a model typical of this great nation.

I came to the river Aude and was immediately fascinated by the feeling of strength of the small city of Carcassonne. Divided into two distinct towns, Ville Basse and the historic Cité, by the Aude, here was a place typical of France and its historic but bloody past.

(Above) In a vineyard outside Carcassone; 1/125 sec. at *f*/8, Hasselblad 500C, 80mm lens.

(Opposite) My model outside the city of Carcassone in the south of France; 1/125 sec. at *f*/8, Hasselblad 500C, 80mm lens.

Shot in an unfinished house outside the walls of Carcassone; 1/125 sec. at *f*/8, Hasselblad 500C, 80mm lens.

(Above) Shot at 1/125 sec. at *f*/8, Hasselblad 500C, 150mm lens.

(Below) Shot at 1/125 sec. at *f*/8, Hasselblad 500C, 80mm lens.

Sacre-Coeur at Montmartre at night; 10 sec. at *f*/8, Hasselblad 500C, 50mm lens.

Carcassonne, held by the nearly forgotten Visigoths after the fall of the Roman Empire and until 724, later was occupied by the Arabs. The Arabs, in turn, lost the area to Pepin the Short.

This is a fortified city, and the fortifications provide a wonderful background for the photographer. Also, the area is noted for its vineyards and is an important wine market. The beauty of the women of Carcassonne should be lengendary. They are not frail creatures, but women with strong features and beautiful bodies.

The day after I found Carcassonne and its grand fortress, I also found my model (and her chaperon). We motored to the edge of the city where I would use both a vineyard and the fortress as a shooting location.

It was then that the trials of modern France were suddenly combined with the tribulations of the past. Coming to a seemingly deserted stone house, I asked what it was. With a look of complete distaste, my model informed me this land had been owned by a Nazi collaborator. The house had been started during the Nazi occupation. The war ended before the building was completed, and the French government placed a restriction on both the land and the building. The collaborator could neither finish it nor sell it. This is truly a home with no future.

My model eagerly accepted the suggestion that she pose in the windows and doors of this shell of a place, with the old fortress visible in the background—thus, linking the present with the near and distant past. I'm particularly fond of these shots; they'll always remind me that Carcassonne is not a dead city but one that shares with France the glories of past and present.

I also like the shot of my model kneeling in a large vineyard, like an Eve looking for a grape instead of an apple. And believe me, this Eve, found in a weaving shop in the ancient city, would turn any Adam's eye.

The fortress in all its grandeur is shown in a shot with my model sitting on an ancient stone wall, the verdant meadow brushed profusely with yellow-centered, white daisies.

I sighed as I put my cameras and equipment in my compact European car. I'd successfully found a city typical of the history of France and a model who fitted the scene superbly.

As I drove back to Paris, never finishing my tour to the Riviera, I congratulated myself for getting out of the glitter of France's "Fun City." As I discovered in most countries I visited, the typical flavor of a country is found in the countryside and the small towns—not in the carnival-paced life of the big city.

A farm girl seated in a wheat field; 1/125 sec. at *f*/11, Hasselblad 500C, 80mm lens.

Belgium

After two days of sitting through auditions in Antwerp and Brussels, I became a little discouraged with my trip to Belgium to photograph a girl typical of that historic and war-weary country. I had always wanted to visit Belgium because of the courage and hardiness of her people.

I was discouraged but not because the girls I had been auditioning were not beautiful. They were, very much so. There had been a steady stream of brunettes, redheads, and blondes—fashion models, photographers' and artists' models, and even a few actresses. They all had the same attributes. All were beautiful and, with a few exceptions, possessed hourglass figures.

My problem was my strong feeling that not one of them was typical of her country and not one was graced with the strength of face or figure I was looking for in my Belgian model.

The fault was mine from the start. During my visits to many countries, I had purposely avoided using professional models, as a rule, because I was looking for women that didn't look like every other model in the world. Let's face it: professional models have much the same look whether it be in New York, London, Paris, or Rome. There's a dull sameness.

Still, I was trapped into looking at professional models when I first started walking the streets of Antwerp. Perhaps, it's because this historic city is a great world diamond center that it attracts beautiful women. They seemed to be everywhere.

I looked and looked and looked. Not one of the stunning creatures had the Belgian look. Leaving the diamond city of Antwerp,

Rimlighting, shooting almost into the sun; 1/125 sec. at *f*/11, Hasselblad 500C, 80mm lens.

(Left) Shot at 1/125 sec. at *f*/11, Hasselblad 500C, 80mm lens. (Right) With the same settings, but a 150mm lens.

Shot at 1/125 sec. at *f*/11, Hasselblad 500C, 80mm lens, into the sun.

I motored to Brussels, the main financial center of this small country. Again, I looked and looked and looked. Beauty after beauty paraded before my inquisitive eyes. I still didn't find what I wanted.

"I'm sorry," I said to a photographer friend, Pierre, as the last of a series of models passed by, "but I just can't seem to find the girl that is, to me, typical of Belgium."

Pierre rolled his dark eyes, gave an eloquent shrug that dismissed this crazy American, and spread his arms wide. "And what are you looking for, my friend? What are you seeking in the Belgian woman?"

"Strength, for that's the word I find synonymous with this country," I replied.

"Ah!" he said. "You must get out into the country then. There are the women of strength."

He was right, of course. The pretty, pampered pets in the cities may have had strength at one time, both in face and in body, but the good life had weakened it. The latest fashions, professional make-up, perfumes, and paint can enhance the beauty of any country girl, but she is no longer the same woman.

I decided to motor through the countryside. It didn't take long to notice the difference. The Ardennes and Meuse Valleys, long noted for their coal industries (now diminishing), the abundant forests in the Sambre-Meuse belt, and the rich grain areas of the country had real people. I found the true strength of Belgium in the weathered, honest, strong faces of the peasants in the rural areas. These people possessed the true spirit of Belgium—the same spirit that drove men to battle the Nazis during World War II, making it possible for the British to escape massacre and withdraw from Dunkirk. These same people, those who survived, made life miserable for the Germans during the latter part of the war.

During my motor tour I found, too, that Belgium is still divided within itself, both by politics and language. The Flemish-speaking Belgians, who speak a variety of dialects or standard Dutch, still cannot live completely at peace with the French-speaking Walloons, and vice versa. Brussels is at least one exception, for here those differences must be ignored to a degree so that the economy of the nation can flourish.

After more days of searching I found the woman I was looking for. She had long, loose, black hair; a solid, honest face, full of strength; and a sturdy body with fine breasts. She was a woman any country would be proud to claim as its own, but, to me, she was typical of Belgium.

My shooting location was a lush field of wheat with a farm in the background. This, too, seemed typical, because three-fifths of the country is under cultivation, despite the fact that a large part of Belgium is rocky terrain and poor agricultural land.

It was about nine o'clock in the morning when my model, her chaperon, and I arrived for the shooting session. But my troubles weren't over yet.

Farmers in Belgium, as in many parts of the United States, must rise early and get their chores finished. I didn't know it, but a reception committee was about to pay its respects.

As my model disrobed and struck a pose in the field of wheat, the thatched roof of the farm cottage in the background, I became aware of the rustling of feet and a strange murmuring. Looking up from the groundglass of my Hasselblad camera, I was surprised to find we had company—a group of farmers and workers stood and watched.

I hadn't asked permission to use the wheat field (and I certainly knew better; a photographer should always get written permission) and had the sudden feeling I was in for a bad time. It never developed! They stood watching for a few minutes, talked quietly among themselves, uttered no word of protest, and soon left us alone.

I didn't take many photos of my Belgian girl. I felt the one in the wheat field was what I wanted. Then, we went to a grove of trees at the edge of the field, and I took some rimlighting shots and semi-silhouettes. We left soon afterwards and saw no further sign of the farmers and workers.

I arrived back in Antwerp later that day and again saw the hourglass figures, painted faces, and high breasts pushing against high fashions. I was glad I'd had sense enough to journey into the country where the strength of Belgium is found.

Luxembourg

In planning the itinerary of my European tour, I purposely put Luxembourg at the bottom of the list. It seemed to me to be one of the most European of all countries, despite its small size and the fact that its population remained under 300,000 until the late 1950's.

But Luxembourg has a long history of playing unwilling host to rulers from other lands. Back in 50 B.C. Luxembourg was the home of a Belgic tribe, the Treveri. Then came the Roman conquest and centuries of conflict under German, Spanish, French, Belgian, and Dutch rule.

The capital city of Luxembourg, or Lutzelburg (little fortress), still has many buildings that reflect its turbulent history. Situated on high cliffs overlooking the river Alzette, this city is one of the most picturesque I've ever photographed. As I walked down the Avenue de la Libèrté to keep an appointment with a photographer friend, Henri, I had already decided to use the historic background of the city as a shooting location. The wonderful bridges with their arches and carvings were perfect for atmosphere.

Later, as Henri and I sat in a small restaurant and talked about my photographic experiences, he asked if it didn't require a lot of optimistic fortitude to pose a nude model in public places without first obtaining official permission from civic authorities.

"My friend, you have posed your nudes in wheat fields, vineyards, castle ruins, and parks in countries where you don't even speak the language. Where do you find the nerve?" he asked, throwing up his hands in wonderment.

The classic lines of the bridge blend gracefully with those of the model; 1/125 sec. at *f*/8, Hasselblad 500C, 80mm lens.

I shrugged and explained, "One thing I learned in the U.S. Army and Air Force, Henri, was this: If you ask permission and the answer is No! you cannot do it at all. But, if you go ahead and do something and then ask permission, it's too late for them to say no."

"Perhaps, but the *gendarmerie* could make it most difficult for you. Aren't you afraid they'll confiscate those beautiful expensive cameras?" he asked, his blue eyes blinking owlishly behind black-framed glasses.

"No, no," I assured him. "I know from experience that if what you have done is entirely legitimate, the authorities and property owners seldom complain even though they'd refuse permission if you asked first."

I didn't know it in the restaurant, but my shooting session in Luxembourg was to be a case in point. I had no difficulty in finding a model I liked, and she provided the chaperon.

I'd found a location that was ideal, one of the city's beautiful parks that had water, bridges, and arches. However, all parks in this old city are much used by the residents, and seldom can you find them unoccupied. Since I had no desire to have a large audience while working, I once again arranged to begin shooting with the first light of dawn.

After I had assembled my cameras and my model had disrobed, I moved around looking for proper angles and lighting. It was then that I discovered we already had company—a gardener with pruning shears was on the job 100 yards away. He saw us, too, but went on with his work as though beautiful nude girls in the park were part of his everyday life.

One of my favorite shots of my Luxembourg model shows her leaning against the entrance to an ornate arched bridge, the texture and carvings making a fine background. A second photo, taken from across the stream and showing the arch of the bridge and the model from the back, is lovely, too. I'm also pleased with the composition of a picture I took with the model sitting on top of the arch.

We moved to the long grass on the bank of the stream where I took two fine shots. One shows the model testing the temperature of the water with her hand; the other captures her in the grass, the blurred arch of the bridge in the background.

We finished the shooting session as quickly as possible with the gardener showing no interest at any time. By the time I had packed my cameras, people were starting to file into the park, and benches near the gate were already fully occupied. As we crossed the bridge

Shot at 1/125 sec. at *f*/11, Hasselblad 500C, 80mm lens.

Also shot at 1/125 sec. at *f*/11, Hasselblad 500C, 80mm lens.

Reaching for the sun; 1/125 sec. at *f*/12.5, Hasselblad 500C, 80mm lens.

Model kneeling in the wet grass; 1/125 sec. at *f*/11, Hasselblad 500C, 80mm lens.

Reflections; 1/125 sec. at *f*/11, Hasselblad 500C, 150mm lens.

that had served both as my model's dressing room and a prop for posing, a nun and her class of children met us, coming to the park for their hour in the sun.

Later, as I described my adventure to Henri, he chuckled and threw his hands wide in his characteristic gesture. "You're a little bit crazy, my friend, but I must admit your methods work."

They seem to—otherwise, most of the pictures in this book would never have been taken.

Ireland

"Thuairim póg, caílín og."

My lips struggled with the Gaelic words.

"Thuairim póg, caílín og."

I leaned forward in the comfort of my plush seat inside the huge silver bird, my lips still struggling, and looked out the window—down, down to the Magic Isle, Ireland. The old cliché is true, I thought, she is a jewel in the ocean. Her many-faceted emerald face sparkled under the probing beams of a brilliant sun.

"Thuairim póg, caílín og."

Why is it, I thought, that a traveler will try to learn a few local phrases when visiting a strange country. More often than not, using them will cause more trouble than pleasure. *Thuairim póg, caílín og* is a good example. It means, "Kiss me, my pretty."

"Fasten your seat belts, please!" The order, delivered in a delightful brogue, snapped me from my reverie. I looked out again and could see Shannon Airport in the distance. My heartbeat quickened as the wheels of the plane feathered the runway and the skreek, skreek of brakes slowed our pace.

". . . a slow approach is wise where true acquaintance is expected," Kate O'Brien admonishes in *My Ireland*. She's talking both of her country and of her people—and she's right.

I was headed for Kate O'Brien's hometown of Limerick, just 20 miles east of the airport, confident I'd find my Irish girl in this historic and romantic city. Sacked by the Danes in 812 and scourged by the Black and Tans in the 1920's, it is an ancient place, shaped

While looking for a new place to shoot, I saw my model through the trees. I turned and took this candid shot focusing on the model and letting the foreground go slightly soft; 1/125 sec. at *f*/11, Hasselblad 500C, 80mm lens.

by centuries of grief, sieges, invasions, strong-willed men, and beautiful women (equally strong-willed).

The drive to the city was all too short. My photographer's eye was kept busy looking for shooting locations. In the distance a religious landmark extended into the blue of the horizon—the spire of St. John's Cathedral. Compared to the city into which the cathedral has thrust its sturdy roots, this Gothic structure is a mere babe, just 100 years old. When you see the spire, you know Limerick is not far off.

During the next few days I wandered around the historic streets, absorbing mood and atmosphere—the Treaty Stone at the end of Thomond Bridge, King John's Castle, St. Mary's Cathedral, Cannock's Clock, King's Island, Whitanmore's Castle, the beautiful Shannon River and its quays, and, everywhere, ivy-covered walls.

I took Kate O'Brien's advice,". . . a slow approach is wise . . . ." I was beginning to get the feel of Limerick and of Ireland.

Then I saw her! Broad shoulders squared in a neat emerald dress, she swung down the sidewalk with easy grace, blue eyes smiling, and a small green handbag swinging at her side. This was no mini-skirted teenybopper. If this Irish girl could, perchance, market her natural look, she'd put fashion designers and cosmeticians out of business the world over.

". . . a slow approach . . . a slow approach . . . ." The words were flashing neon warnings in my mind as I pursued her.

Three days later, accompanied by a pleasant but no-nonsense chaperon, we drove out of Limerick, headed for one of those ivy-covered walls I had decided to use for a shooting location. I had been blessed with sunshine for four straight days, but now the windshield wipers swished rhythmically as we drove through a steady drizzle in the gray light of early morning. Our spirits, however, were bright —a combination of Irish coffee and anticipation of adventure ahead.

As I scrambled from the small car and wrestled with camera case, tripod, and gadget bags, my Irish girl and her chaperon remained in the car. The fresh air, cleansed by the rain, carried the fragrance of heather and cleared my head for the job to be done. The ivy-covered wall looked like a perfect setting.

While bent over my Hasselblad camera, I was startled by a series of exuberant shrieks. Turning, I saw my model cavorting like a young colt suddenly released to green pasture. She was dressed only in the jewels of warm raindrops. Surely, she's a leprechaun, I thought, one of the fairies of Ireland—a *Tuatha da Danaan.*

Although she was not a professional model, my Irish lass proved to have a natural instinct for posing. I gave no directions, merely followed her with my camera, clicking the shutter steadily, changing lens openings and shutter speeds, and switching camera backs. She, too, felt an affinity for the ivy-covered wall, gravitating to it immediately.

In these two pictures my model knelt for a second, and since a light rain was falling, she adjusted her hair slightly to wring out some of the water before she struck the pose at the right; 1/125 sec. at *f*/8, Hasselblad 500C, 80mm lens.

Using the ivy for a background, she sat on a large stone and framed herself nicely for a three-quarter shot; she stood and reached to pick a leaf, the rain coursing down her body; she partly framed herself beside a bush, and I threw her and the background out of focus on my groundglass; then, she dropped to her knees and started to untangle the end of her hair, bedraggled by the rain.

I ran out of film and had to change camera backs. When I looked up again, she was gone. I looked around and saw the chaperon still sitting in the car, out of the rain. She pointed to a clearing in the trees nearby. My trousers were soon soaked to the knees as I waded through the long grass.

My model found this spider's web and became engrossed in the tiny drops of rain embedded like jewels in the web. I fired these shots in rapid succession as she gazed intently at the web; 1/125 sec. at *f*/8, Hasselblad 500C, 80mm lens.

(Above) An enlargement of the shot on p. 56, printed a bit softer.

(Opposite) Another example of selective focus; 1/250 sec. at *f*/5.6, Hasselblad 500C, 250mm lens focused on the berries.

I stopped, breathless with fascination. God, I prayed, "Please don't let her move." She was seated, a jeweled spider's web hanging on fine suspension cables in front of her face. I clicked off shot after shot but she was totally unaware of my presence. Her china blue eyes were filled with a look of childlike wonder. I finished off the roll, lit a cigarette, and shifted my weight from foot to foot, feeling awkward and uncomfortable. I was reluctant to invade the privacy of her moment. Finally, I gave a gentle cough; the spell was broken. A gleaming smile brought us back together.

That night, at Shannon Airport, we stood, making small talk in the lobby. She had come to see me off, and now it was time to go.

"*Thuairim póg, caílín og,*" I stuttered, my face flaming. Her lips curving in a smile, she gave my fingers a final squeeze and turned to walk away. She didn't understand Gaelic—I suppose.

Italy

In 20 countries I had photographed nudes in every conceivable locale—the woods, farmers' fields and vineyards, public parks and beaches, abandoned houses, or wherever an intriguing setting and model merged before my lens. Not once had I faced the challenge of a property owner, constable, or *gendarme.* Although I felt that I could prove the esoteric qualities of my work, I wasn't anxious to be hauled before a magistrate if I could avoid it.

The minute my wife and I landed in Italy, I had a premonition of trouble. This was one of the few countries in which a model had been arranged for in advance and, by logic, everything should move along with exceptional ease. Yet, for some indefinable reason, I felt that we were in for trouble; not knowing its nature or when to expect it made me edgy.

Instead of arranging an immediate shooting session with Angela, the model, I stalled. Roll after roll of black-and-white and color film went into producing stock photos of the Tower of Pisa and the alabaster carvers of Pisa, the Palace of San Marco Plaza and the streets of Venice, the Italian villages and countryside, and the city flea markets. I studied the Collosseum in Rome and rejected the notion of using it as a locale for nudes. It would be too risky at any time of day or night. The Memorial to Vittorio Emmanuele in Rome known as "The Wedding Cake" didn't appeal to me either. It was in the museum of Lateran that I had a flash of inspiration when an interesting group of artifacts caught my eye. They were from the ruins of Ostia, an ancient city that had once flourished at the mouth of the Tiber river. Ostia was a port city said to have been the first colony ever founded by Rome.

The modern road from Rome to Ostia follows traces of the ancient Via Ostiensis in a southwesterly direction for 14 miles. As I approached the parts of the city that have been excavated from the sandy soil, I could visualize the vanished harbor where, in 62 A.D. alone, no less than 200 cargo-laden ships were sunk by the treacherous winds from the open sea.

With the exception of Pompeii, Ostia is the finest example in Italy of a city of the Roman period. Here it was that the worship of Vulcan produced some of the priests who became Roman senators. It was a city known to Trajan, Caesar, Claudius, and Nero, scourged by the Punic and Gothic wars, and, finally, abandoned to ravaging pirates.

I knew at a glance that this was the locale in which I wanted to shoot, but although the excavated portions covered a large area, there were tourists and guards everywhere. It was while driving around the city that I noticed a new fence being built to surround an excavated area. At one spot in the rear of the area, the fence wasn't quite completed. A narrow opening in the fence gave me an idea.

By six o'clock the next morning I was back at Ostia, accompanied by my wife and Angela. I squeezed my rented Fiat through the tiny opening in the fence and parked. Then, the three of us walked half a mile into the main streets of the city. A few minutes later I was photographing Angela beside the pillars and on the ornate mosaic floors of the temple buildings. The soft gray morning light flattered her body from all angles, as I moved from one vantage point to another. Pausing only long enough to compose, shoot, and advance the film, I exposed one Hasselblad magazine of film after another as time seemed to stand still.

About seven-thirty a car suddenly appeared out of nowhere and roared past the spot where I was standing upright on a wall. I fancied I saw men in uniform in the car, but as it sped into the distance, I had the consolation of knowing that the occupants of the car couldn't have seen Angela on the other side of the wall. I resumed shooting until I heard a faint crunching of wheels in the sand. It was as though the car were approaching slowly and quietly this time to get as close as possible without being noticed.

"You better get dressed," I told Angela. Accompanied by my wife, she scurried to an alcove where she had left her clothing.

Venetian shopkeepers commuting to work in the early morning hours; 1/60 sec. at *f*/11, Hasselblad 500C, 80mm lens.

(Above) Colosseum at two o'clock in the morning; 2 min. at *f*/16, Hasselblad 500C, 50mm lens.

(Opposite) Marble and flesh form a striking contrast; 1/60 sec. at *f*/8, Hasselblad 500C, 80mm lens.

The women were barely out of sight when the car poked its nose around a wall and stopped a few feet away. Two men in guards' uniforms got out and approached me. In Italian, spiced with fractured English, the taller guard said pointedly, "Where are the girls?"

I heard myself hemming and hawing, wondering how they knew about the girls. Both men started walking toward the alcove. I knew that Angela hadn't had enough time to get dressed. "Wait, wait!" I said.

The tall one said sternly, "You have broken the law. You must all go to the manager's office to await the police."

"*Un momento, merci, bitte,* please?" I protested. "Let me take a picture of you first, yes?"

"What? A picture of us?"

"Yes, yes. I need a picture of you!"

"No. It is not allowed."

"But I promise your faces won't show. You may turn your backs toward me. I want a picture of you at your work, guarding the walls."

They hesitated. "Well, just one." They walked over to an opening in the walls.

Somehow it took eternities for me to find the right angle, direct them to the proper poses, and focus. I talked endlessly. After eight or ten minutes, they grew impatient. Just as I was sure they'd flare into anger, my wife and Angela walked up, their faces aglow with smiles.

The scene in the manager's office was loud and dramatic. There was much waving of arms and questions directed with accusing glares. My wife and I didn't understand what they were saying. Finally, I asked Angela what charges they were pressing and what they were offering as proof.

"They have proof," she said, "but maybe the manager will drop charges if you pay willingly."

I reached for my traveler's checks. "How much will it take to square it?" I asked, hoping it wouldn't exceed 20 American dollars.

Angela questioned the manager. They began to argue. As her voice rose, his jaw grew as rigid as if carved from Ostia marble. With a disdainful shrug, Angela abruptly gave up.

"He won't settle for anything less than full price," she told me. "If you don't pay the regular tourist admission price for three tickets, he will call the police."

I allowed my model to wander around freely, and I captured this candid; 1/60 sec. at *f*/8, Hasselblad 500C, 80mm lens.

(Above) The model makes a striking figure silhouetted in an archway, which must have led down to either an ancient catacomb or storage cellar; 1/60 sec. at *f*/11, Hasselblad 500C, 80mm lens.

(Opposite) Shot at 1/60 sec. at *f*/8, Hasselblad 500C, 80mm lens.

Flabbergasted, I paid a trivial admission fee for three tickets, accepted a tongue lashing for gate crashing, and departed in hopes that the incident was ended.

The next day, my wife and I boarded an Italian airliner bound for Athens. Before leaving Rome, we had arranged to pick up a rented Volkswagen at the airport in Athens. Rome seemed far behind as we entered the Athens terminal building. Then, the loudspeaker blared, "Passenger Stewart Rothman will please contact the stewardess. This is urgent. Passenger Stewart Rothman will please. . . ."

I located the stewardess. She said briefly, "Kindly do not leave the terminal. A car from the Italian Embassy is coming to pick you up."

That did it. I felt beads of sweat begin to soak my shirt collar. My scalp prickled and I fancied that my hair was turning hoarier by the second. What other laws had I broken in Italy? I was safe in Greece, but most of our luggage and my camera equipment were still in our hotel in Rome. There was nothing else to do but return to Italy and face the music. How clever the manager at Ostia had been to make notes of our passports. Now he would no doubt find a pretext to press charges for more money. Would I stand a chance in an Italian court? I had some reservations on that score.

We waited ten minutes. Nervously, I approached the stewardess. "There's been a mistake," I said. "We aren't expecting a car from the Italian Embassy."

"Oh yes, Mr. Rothman. It was very urgent, very explicit. You are to wait for the Embassy car."

A moment later a man in a neat black suit approached me. I could see no insignia on his policeman's cap. He said, "Mr. Rothman, Steward?"

"No, it's Mr. Stu Rothman. Perhaps a mistake . . .?"

"I am from the rent-a-car agency, Mr. Steward. I have brought your Volkswagen."

The thought ran through my mind that we could hop into the Volkswagen and make a run for the nearest border, but what

(Top) I talked the guards into posing for this photo while my model dressed. Since they had seen only her head above a wall, they did not know she was nude; 1/60 sec. at *f*/8, Hasselblad 500C, 80mm lens.

(Bottom) Shot at 1/60 sec. at *f*/8, Hasselblad 500C, 80mm lens.

(Above) Ruins of the Roman Forum; 1/125 sec. at *f*/12.5, Hasselblad 500C, 50mm lens.

(Opposite) Night scene along the canals of Venice; 1 sec. at *f*/2.8, Hasselblad 500C, 80mm lens.

border? And what difference would that make if they wanted me in Rome? "I'm very sorry," I said, putting on the best face I could behind my beard and sunglasses, "but it seems I won't need the Volkswagen today."

"Oh?"

"No. I haven't the foggiest idea why, but the Italian Embassy is sending a car for us. I suppose I've committed a minor infraction of regulations or something. They had me paged on the loudspeaker."

The man burst into laughter. "Oh, that! It's nothing. I was the one who had you paged. You see, if I call the airport and say we are sending a car to meet you, they sometimes forget to broadcast the message. But," he tapped his forehead and winked, "if I say the Italian Embassy is sending the car, they never forget. Always, they broadcast very loud, very clear."

* * *

I'll never forget my first afternoon in Athens—the azure skies, the shining white buildings, and the smiling people. Nor will I forget my first night in Athens—the wonderful food and the music that starts out slowly and softly, then rises on a throbbing beat to a crescendo that launches your spirits into space. At least, I say the music does it. My wife insists that the Greek wine helps. At any rate, I distinctly remember toasting, several times, the man I'd misjudged at Ostia and dedicating a few more toasts to the Italian Embassy and the rent-a-car agency in Athens.

Greece

When my wife and I flew from Rome to "case" Greece ahead of time, there were moments at the airport when I thought my beard was going to change to instant-white. Now, looking out my hotel window at the ancient fortified hill known as the Acropolis, I tried to remember what I had learned about Greece in school.

Athens, Sparta, Olympia, and Thebes, as I recalled, were originally city-states of mixed European ancestry. As an independent community, each had its own dialect, government, social system, laws, gods, and customs. Their one common denominator, according to the poet Herodotus, was poverty.

In visiting Athens and Salonika, I found city life much the same as in Tampa or Minneapolis. Yet Greece definitely has customs, characteristics, and traditions that set it uniquely apart from other countries.

In the self-governing community of Mount Athos, for example, neither a woman nor a female animal has ever been permitted to enter. I learned about the Greek sense of humor when two acquaintances in a *tavernas* offered a straight-faced suggestion that I visit Mount Athos in search of nude models.

The *tavernas* of Greece are the hubs of social relaxation where people enjoy savory chopped meat topped with lemon sauce and wrapped in grape leaves. They drink great quantities of *retsina* (wine mixed with pine sap) or a liquor called *ouzo*. Both the music and the patrons were impulsive. As the mood struck them, they danced, men and women together, or men with men, in what seemed to me to be

View of the Parthenon from the eighth floor of my hotel by day and by night; 1/125 sec. at *f*/8, Hasselblad 500C, 250mm lens. Photo on pp. 78–79, shot at 1 min. at *f*/11, 500mm lens.

largely improvised gyrations. Some of the women were strikingly beautiful, but they reminded me of beautiful women I'd seen in many other lands. Without make-up or costume or jewelry, they could pass for tourists from almost anywhere.

In widening my search, I found attractive women everywhere—in vineyards, on mountain trails, in factories, gathered around the community radio in isolated rural communities, and in the flea markets. Almost always I could (or thought I could) distinguish traits that identified specific ways of life. Something about a girl indicated "peasant," "shopgirl," "housewife," "college girl," or "entertainer." But girls with "labels," real or imaginary, were what I didnt want. I wanted a composite. Someone who, to me, epitomized the "Grecian woman."

I found her in a shop, when I discovered that the high counters in many of the stores were causing me to misjudge the sex of the shopkeeper. Seeing just a head behind the counter, I found myself inventing excuses to slide around the corner of a counter to obtain a fuller view of the shopkeeper. That was often the only way I could tell whether I was talking to a boy or a girl. Because of their astonishingly similar features and hair styles, my first guess was wrong as often as it was right.

The girl I hoped would become my model listened patiently to her prospective chaperon's translation of my objectives. As she shook her head, my hopes faded. Then the chaperon said, "She agrees. Where will the posing take place?"

I had already chosen the terrain. I explained that I felt that the girl's high cheek bones and boyish figure typified a form of beauty I had rarely seen outside Greece and that the Plains of Attica would be a perfect setting. She seemed neither pleased nor flattered by my compliments. If she was moved by my suggestion that she and the Plains of Attica "belonged" to each other in my artistically romantic concept, she didn't show it. Perhaps she cared nothing for ancient Greek history. Maybe she thought I'd been tippling the *retsina* bottle. We arranged a time and place for meeting the next morning. Then, she walked back behind her counter without another word.

The wind swept over the Plains of Attica at dawn just as it had done for centuries. The angular trees and thorny shrubs were exactly suited to emphasizing the lines and bones of the girl's figure by virtue of stark contrast. It was a bleak and pitiless stretch of wasteland with only a solitary figure to symbolize the soft warmth of human flesh and blood.

The inside and outside views of the Erechtheum on the Acropolis in Athens; 1/125 sec., Hasselblad 500C; (above) *f*/8, 50mm lens; (opposite) *f*/11, 80mm lens.

The boyish facial features of my Greek model blended perfectly with the ancient trees on the wind-swept plains of Attica; 1/125 sec. at *f*/11, Hasselblad 500C, 150mm lens.

This is the only photograph in this book taken with a 35mm camera. All five of my Hasselblad magazines were empty at one time, and while I was loading them my model struck this relaxed pose. I immediately grabbed my Nikon and caught this pose; 1/125 sec. at *f*/8, Nikon F, 43–86mm zoom lens set at maximum of 86mm.

Model relaxes after posing for several hours; 1/125 sec. at *f*/11, Hasselblad 500C, 150mm lens.

As I moved from one camera position to another, I kept wondering what the girl was thinking. Was she, too, visualizing this landscape as it must have been 2,500 years ago? Did she realize that the Plains of Attica were once the proud mecca of pomp and pageantry—the place that gave birth to the brilliancy, grandeur, and mighty accomplishments that came to be spoken of as the "Golden Age" of Pericles?

I asked the chaperon if she knew the history of the area. Her face and tone were expressionless as she dug in her purse for a cigarette and match. "Greece is different now," she said with a shrug.

Spain

The large airliner circled Prat airport, seven miles west of Barcelona, and I had a feeling I'd come to Spain at the wrong time. Every seat in the plane was filled. It was obvious, too, that most of them contained tourists. If there was one thing I didn't need around when I photographed a Spanish nude, it was a group of curious, smirking tourists and their 35mm cameras or super 8mm movie cameras.

I sighed as I glanced out the window and saw the beauty of the Llobregat plain with the Tibidabo looming in the background. Barcelona nestled like an ancient jewel between the rivers Besós and Llobregat on a gentle slope facing the Mediterranean. I'd chosen this beautiful old city because of its history, surrounding area, and the fierce independence of its people.

The plane landed, and I took a car to my hotel, noting with mounting irritation that the streets were flooded with humanity. An exploratory walk later that day confirmed my fears. I rented a car and drove around—tourists, tourists, tourists—everywhere you looked were tourists. I'd have my job cut out for me.

In this land of clicking castanets, snapping fingers, and the colorful, electrifying six-eight time of the *fandango,* I had expected some difficulty in locating a model to be my Spanish nude. I found this would be the least of my worries. I had found her, complete with chaperon, within a day. Now, the problem would be to find a location where we would have some measure of privacy, both for my photography and my model and her ever-present chaperon.

Nude partially shaded by the trees creating a semi-silhouette; 1/125 sec. at *f*/8, Hasselblad 500C, 50mm lens.

Barcelona has all the color, mood, and atmosphere any photographer could ask for, to say nothing of writers and artists. There are literally thousands of locations where I could set up my cameras and take charming photos. Nature and man have fashioned fascinating backgrounds for picture-taking. The trouble was that tourists found these places fascinating too, and were out in full force, Instamatic cameras swinging from their wrists or 35mm cameras hanging from their necks.

Many of their favorite places wouldn't do as a location for my type of photo. Tourists were fascinated by the Universidad Literaria founded in 1430, restored in 1841, and enlarged in the 1950's. Built on the lower slopes, it's near the royal palace of Pedralbes. I was surprised to learn that Barcelona was a seat of learning long before 1430. The Church of the Holy Family in the northwest sector of the city, a magnificent and unique structure with its many steeples, always draws tourists, and certainly did during my stay.

The waterfront, whether quays or beach, can usually be used as a good location for the photographer. The hurry and flurry of the harbor of Barcelona is no exception, with its two breakwaters and floating dock. This setting was fine for postcard and calendar photography but hardly appropriate for nudes—and tourists continued to be a problem.

I decided I'd have to get out into the countryside, or at least to the edge of Barcelona. As I drove around I was thrilled with the adobe buildings, their textures and colors. These would make perfect backgrounds. The tourists thought so, too, and swarmed around the area. To make matters even worse, the natives seemed to enjoy the antics of the tourists, and, now, the natives were getting in the way.

Perhaps, I thought, if I go to the province of Barcelona, I'll be able to get away from both the tourists and the natives.

The scenery was breathtaking, as I motored through the valley of the Llobregat. I visited *Plana de Vich,* famed for its stock-raising, and I crossed the river Ter. In the west I was impressed with the extensive grapevines of *Plá de Bages,* the northern limit of viticulture in the province.

The province of Barcelona is flanked by the mountainous *Guilleriás,* an area famous for its banditry. In fact, the Spanish *Guilleriás* area has given to the world a word that indicates a particularly nasty type of fighting, guerrilla warfare. Paradoxically, the Spanish do not call such warriors guerrillas; they called themselves *partidos,* or partisans.

(Top and lower left) Overlooking Innsbruck in Austria. Ektachrome Professional Daylight film, 1/125 sec. at *f*/12.5, Hasselblad, 150mm lens. (Lower right) High in the Swiss Alps. Ektachrome Type S film, 1/125 sec. at *f*/16, Hasselblad, 80mm lens.

(Top) One of my favorite models, the Austrian girl. Ektachrome Professional Daylight film, 1/125 sec. at *f*/8, Hasselblad, 150mm lens. (Bottom) Dew drops on a spider web and my Irish beauty. Ektacolor Type S film, 1/125 sec. at *f*/5.6, Hasselblad, 150mm lens.

Three nuns on the bridge to Chateau Comtal in Carcassonne. Ektachrome Professional Daylight film, 1/25 sec. at *f*/11, Hasselblad, 50mm lens.

CABARET
CABARET
PIGALL'S
PIGALL'S
REVUE
LES
LES PLUS
DU MONDE

(Top left) Place Pigalle, Paris. Ektachrome Type S Professional film, one second at *f*/12.5, Hasselblad, 80mm lens. (Bottom left) The Eiger, as seen from Grindlewald. Ektachrome Professional Daylight film, 1/125 sec. at *f*/12.5, Hasselblad, 50mm lens. (Above) The Spanish model reaching for a dried fern. Ektacolor Type S film, 1/125 sec. at *f*/8, Hasselblad, 80mm lens.

At a bridge in Luxembourg. Ektachrome Professional Daylight film, 1/125 sec. at *f*/11, Hasselblad, 80mm lens.

(Top) My Austrian model sculpted into a rock outcropping. (Lower left) Towering trees and a lovely woman. (Both) Ektachrome Professional Daylight film, 1/125 sec. at *f*/12.5, Hasselblad, 80mm lens. (Lower right) "The Golden Girl." My Belgian model in a wheat field. Ektacolor Type S film, 1/125 sec. at *f*/8, Hasselblad, 150mm lens.

The Danish girl and diamonds on the water. Ektacolor Type S film, 1/125 sec. at *f*/16, Hasselblad, 150mm lens.

Both of these backlit subjects were shot at 1/125 sec. at *f*/8, Hasselblad 500C, 50mm lens.

(Above) My model relaxes as she digs her toes into the warm sand; 1/125 sec. at *f*/11, Hasselblad 500C, 80mm lens.

(Opposite) The early morning sun filtering through the trees caused this striking effect; 1/125 sec. at *f*/11, Hasselblad 500C, 80mm lens.

Both of these shots were made at 1/125 sec. at *f*/11, Hasselblad 500C, 80mm lens.

Reaching toward a tall palm, my model reveals graceful, flowing lines. The low morning sun through the long grass created the delicate patterns on the model's back; 1/60 sec. at *f*/11, Hasselblad 500C, 80mm lens.

Although not particularly afraid of *partidos* in these mountains, I decided the terrain was too rugged to be used as a shooting location—shooting a camera, that is. I was sure my model wouldn't take too kindly to this rugged area, and she might be afraid of bandits.

Driving back to the capital city of the province of Barcelona, I spotted a number of olive groves and decided that one of these would have to serve as my background.

My model and I started out the next morning, shortly after dawn. It was to be a long day. We found plenty of olive groves, plus a multitude of tourists and curious natives. We drove for hours and hours, enjoying the scenery, the conversation, a delicious lunch, and fine wines, but it seemed we'd never find a suitable location.

Perhaps the luck of the gods favored me that day. When we finally found an olive grove with a secluded spot screened by ferns and shrubbery, the sun was beginning to set. The filtered light was perfect.

I took advantage of the lighting and the shrubbery to create photos with dramatic shadows and highlights. Back and rimlighting seemed particularly appropriate. My model proved to be a natural, completely at ease in her surroundings and seemingly oblivious to the clicking shutter and my constant hopping around. I was especially pleased with a shot of her by a green olive tree, her body in shadow but rimlighted by a low sun. Another favorite shows her reclining against the trunk of the evergreen, while still another shows the model sitting and facing the sun, her right breast highlighted, while her back is in open shadow.

Although pressed for time because we'd found a location so late in the afternoon, we managed to get some good shots.

Driving to Prat airport the next day, I vowed to return to Spain again—in the off-tourist season—if there is such a time.

A hay field just outside Amsterdam; 1/125 sec. at *f*/12.5, Hasselblad 500C, 150mm lens. Photo on pp. 98–99 was shot at the same settings.

Holland

It's a photographer's dream, I thought, as I stood in Amsterdam's Damplein square waiting patiently for a former Miss Amsterdam, who was to serve as my Dutch model. Holland—land of dikes, canals, polders, windmills, tulips, and famous paintings—is exceptionally beautiful.

I glanced at my wristwatch; still another 15 minutes. The National Monument, a memorial to those who fought and died in World War II, towered above me. As always, couples, individuals, and small groups stood around the monument, the older ones probably reliving those days of terror during the German occupation.

Across the square was the Palladian style Royal Palace. Although built during a period from 1648 to 1655, it wasn't used as a palace until 1808. What history this old part of the city might describe, if it could only speak!

I had already met and talked with the former Miss Amsterdam and had decided to do my shooting in and around this capital of the Netherlands. As usual, when I visit a country new to me, I spend a few days walking and motoring to get to know the physical layout of the city and to learn about its history.

Amsterdam is in northern Holland, giving access to the sea through the waterways of the Rhine. A small fishing village at one time, Amsterdam was founded among swamps and stretches of water. It was first mentioned as a town in 1275. Now a well-planned city, it is, also, one literally built on piles.

Model sitting among the weeds in a park in Amsterdam; 1/125 sec. at *f*/11, Hasselblad 500C, 80mm lens.

Luigi Guicciardini was right, I thought, this is "the Venice of the North." Divided into two main sections by the canalized Amstel River, it is subdivided by 50 canals into 70 islands, connected by 500 bridges.

While I was looking around the square for my Dutch model, my attention quickened as I saw her walking past a stone lion on a circular pedestal. Her long dark hair flowed down the back of her light raincoat. It wasn't raining but the sky was overcast and the air felt raw. She waved as she spotted me, tossed her mane, and quickened her pace. Together we stood, took one last look at the war memorial, and headed for my small car.

I had chosen a spot on a dike for my shooting location, one that had an abundance of water nearby, verdant grass, and, of course, a windmill in the background. After all, how could you capture the atmosphere of Holland without a windmill.

As we drove through the city she pointed out some of the old landmarks—the Oude Kerk of St. Nicholas, built in 1300; the Nieuwe Kerk of 1408 vintage; the Westerkerk, Rembrandt's burial place, built in 1631 and boasting the highest tower in Amsterdam, 282 feet; the 18th century red brick homes with their high pointed, sloping gables in the old part of the city; and the equally beautiful architecture in the newer section. I was impressed with the beauty of the many elm and lime trees, painting the streets with bold strokes of color.

Finally, we arrived at the location I had chosen, a picturesque setting probably used for many calendar and postcard pictures, to say nothing of being a favorite haunt for artists. I soon found proof of this: spatters of Antwerp blue, emerald green, alizarin crimson, Mars yellow, and a host of other colors marked a spot where an artist had been carefree with his paints.

My model disrobed in the car and proved a little shy when she first emerged. Short and sturdy, her figure was perfect for the setting I had chosen. Soon her shyness evaporated and, under the watchful eyes of her chaperon, I began shooting.

Several of the photographs I took during this session could have been taken in almost any country. They show the former Miss Amsterdam sitting in high grass partly shielded by sprigs of timothy and wild oats, her long hair adding greatly to the effectiveness of the scene. In one she sits in profile, filtered sun softly outlining her face and lending a mystique to her pensive expression. This is one of my favorites.

The model gazes out to sea as she reclines on the dyke just outside Amsterdam; both shot at 1/125 sec. at *f*/11, Hasselblad 500C, 80mm lens.

Model shyly dipping her toe in the chill morning waters; 1/125 sec. at *f*/8, Hasselblad 500C, 150mm lens.

It was she who told me, with a touch of pride, that her country had been winning the battle with the relentless sea, particularly since World War II. The Free Frisians had started it in the first century A.D. when they built mounds to protect the land against tidal rises. Even today, four-fifths of the Netherlands is below sea level, with dikes and polders staving off the rising of surging waters.

The broken stone of the dike seemed a natural setting for a pose, with the marsh grass and blue water in the background. My model agreed to try, although with an apparent lack of enthusiasm. We tried one shot, but since she couldn't find physical comfort sitting on the sharp-edged rock, we changed locations.

The new site was much better. She sat in the green grass looking across the calm canal to a windmill on the other side. Wild ducks proved cooperative and moved into the picture to improve the composition and atmosphere. This, perhaps, is the photo most typical of the Netherlands, the model's nude figure adding grace of innocence.

It was quite by accident that I obtained another of my favorites. We had finished shooting for the day, and I was preparing to pack my cameras and gear. My Dutch girl, no longer shy and relishing the freedom from confining clothes, wandered through the swamp grass to the edge of the water where she found a small sand beach. I grabbed a camera with a long lens and clicked off a shot just as she poked a toe in the water. Possibly, the composition could have been better if I'd had more time to get in position, but I didn't want to spoil the spontaneity of the scene. It's one that still brings back fond memories of my visit to the Netherlands and the magic city of Amsterdam.

A scene from Grindlewald looking out toward the Eiger; 1/125 sec. at *f*/8, K2 filter, Hasselblad 500C, 80mm lens.

Switzerland

I know I'm not the first to describe Switzerland as a tiny "jewel" in the heart of Europe, but I can vouch for the truth of this statement. Never before have I seen such ruggedly picturesque settings so beautifully maintained. The lakes, the mountains, the hotels and bars, the roads, and even the "local color" are so orderly and proper that one wonders where the reality leaves off and the synthetic begins. Upon arriving in Switzerland, you sense instantly that the populated areas of the country are keenly tourist-conscious and tourist-oriented. But can anyone dye some lakes azure blue and others emerald green? Can anyone paint and sculpt snow on the Alps, or daub rosy cheeks on the children, or command a peasant's leathery face to crinkle into a smile when a stranger comes upon him unexpectedly on a backcountry mountainside farm? When he insists upon sharing his supper of brown bread, cheese, and mountain-grown vegetables with you (with flagons of tart wine pressed from the grapes of his own vineyard), can you suspect he is a "goodwill department" employee of the Swiss government? I doubt it.

I'm also at a loss to explain just where Swiss reality merges into and becomes replaced by facade. It's like stopping at a souvenir stand at an American Indian reservation and buying "genuine" Indian handicrafts. You are afraid to look at the tiny label lest it read, "Made in Japan."

As cities of exquisite beauty in landscaping, statues, and culture, I was greatly impressed with Geneva and Lucerne. Photographing their lakefronts, bustling with excursion and pleasure boats against a backdrop of snowy Alps, I made serious dents in my available film

Scenes at the top of the Jungfrauyoch, which is the saddle connecting the Eiger, Monch, and the Jungfrau; 1/125 sec. at *f*/8, G15 filter (orange), Hasselblad 500C, 80mm lens.

The hotel at Kleine Sheidegg with a cog-wheel train heading through the Eiger to the Jungfrauyoch at the top of the range; 1/125 sec. at *f*/11, K2 filter, Hasselblad 500C, 50mm lens.

supplies. As locales for photographing Swiss nudes, they left me as cold as the distant glaciers.

The same was true of picturesque Zurich. Like Geneva, it is a cosmopolitan crossroads of the world. You have but to stroll along the lakefront to see rows of flags of nations you didn't know existed. Orientals, occidentals, Africans, South Americans, people with totally unfamiliar costumes and tongues converge upon Switzerland, which is socially as well as militarily neutral.

In German-speaking Zurich you learn that the original inhabitants were lake dwellers who built their homes on stilts in the water as a means of defense. In southeastern Switzerland most people speak Italian. In the Geneva area of southwestern Switzerland, French is the everyday language. With a mere sprinkling of understanding of any of these languages, I had to stick with English. Fortunately, the Swiss who deal with tourists have had the foresight to add English (and sometimes three or four more languages) to their vocabularies. Here, as everywhere else in Europe, I got along nicely with plain gestures and patience.

Models in the major tourist cities of Switzerland were easy to find, but useless to me. They were too cosmopolitan by environment, if not by birth, to typify the native Swiss female as I conceived her. Abandoning the cities, I headed inland toward the heart of the Alps. Here, despite the commercialism one finds in the areas that have acquired tastes for beer cans, yoyos, and the American dollar, one can still find more or less unspoiled natives, especially during the off-tourist season.

At Interlaken you are at an altitude of 1,500 feet. By car or train you reach Grindlewald at 3,000 feet. Now, by narrow gauge, cog-wheel train you begin to ascend slopes that make delicate females faint and strong men blanch. If you start to think what would happen if the cogs or cables on these slopes failed, refrain! It would be messy indeed.

Up by cog to Kleine Scheidegg brings you to 7,000 feet and thinning air. Now, you are merely at the feet of the snow-capped mountains, Eiger, Monch, and Jungfrau. I particularly liked the Jungfrau area. The name, incidently, means "young woman," and the perky twin peaks are self-explanatory.

To find a model in the hinterlands of Switzerland was anything but easy. It took my utmost patience and persuasiveness, but at last I succeeded and, with chaperon in tow, managed by cog and by foot to reach a secluded spot. Trains looked like crawling ants on the Al-

My bashful model in Switzerland agreed to pose only if her face did not show; both shot at 1/125 sec. at *f*/11, Hasselblad 500C, 80mm lens.

Both photos were shot at 1/125 sec. at *f*/11, Hasselblad 500C, 80mm lens.

pine railway far below. Herds of sheep, goats, and Swiss cattle grazed on the bright green shoulders of precipitous cliffs. Across the valley Jungfrau thrust her twin snow-capped peaks into the azure skies.

My model, who had never posed before, reminded me of Reubens' subjects. She was graceful and agile in her movements but of generous proportions. I liked her because she typified, far better than the svelt showgirl-types in the cities, the stocky essence of Swiss femininity. Broad of shoulder like the Alpine peasant and sturdy of thigh like the Alpine huntsman or forester, she seemed to me to epitomize a people who had found sanctuary, homes, and an unpretentiously simple way of life. I would not trade this model for the most gorgeous actress Switzerland has ever produced. When twilight put an end to the shooting, I was satisfied with her type of beauty in her Switzerland. She and the rugged terrain seemed to me to have a certain indescribable empathy for one another. They "belonged" together.

The model relaxes in her father's garden; 1/125 sec. at *f*/11, Hasselblad 500C, 80mm lens.

Liechtenstein

In Austria they tell of the man from Liechtenstein who had always wanted to see his country from the air. To do so, he boarded an airliner in Austria and managed to get a fine seat next to a window. When the intercom crackled and the pilot said, "We are now passing over the Austrian border into Liechtenstein," the man excitedly pressed his nose against the glass. Suddenly, he sneezed violenty. With a forefinger jammed beneath his nose, he looked out the window just in time to hear, "and, now, we are passing over the Rhine into Switzerland."

Sandwiched between Austria and Switzerland, Liechtenstein is the fourth smallest country in the world. Its total population of 17,000 live mainly in the valley of the Rhine in an area eight square miles smaller than the District of Columbia. Famous for its finely engraved postage stamps, the people speak German, use Swiss money, and have blended certain elements of the cultures of both countries. Since I doubted that I would find a nude model willing to be photographed outdoors in Liechtenstein, I was resigned to photographing striking examples of architecture, both old and new.

It was a visit to the home of an artist friend that suddenly fired my hopes of finding a model in this tiny principality. My friend showed me several sketches and paintings he'd made of a lovely model. She was obviously in the prime of young maidenhood, and in ways that I somehow couldn't put into words, she seemed to me to symbolize both the youth and the maturity of Liechtenstein.

"Could I possibly meet her and perhaps persuade her to pose for me?" I asked.

(Above) Shot at 1/125 sec. at *f*/11, Hasselblad 500C, 150mm lens.

(Opposite) Intricate patterns created by the sun filtering through the trees; 1/125 sec. at *f*/8, Hasselblad 500C, 150mm lens.

(Above) A double exposure giving an ethereal aura to the photo with the ghostlike massive tree drifting overhead. Exposure for "ghost": 1/250 sec. at *f*/11, Hasselblad 500C, 150mm lens; re-exposure for main subject: 1/125 sec. at *f*/11, Hasselblad 500C, 80mm lens.

(Opposite) Shot at 1/125 sec. at *f*/11, Hasselblad 500C, 80mm lens.

"Perhaps," my artist friend replied, exchanging a glance with his wife. "Can you join us for dinner tonight?"

At dinner, I met the model, their 17-year-old daughter.

The subject of age deserves a word of caution whenever one photographs nudes. The ages at which a model can legally sign a valid release of her own vary from 18 to 21 years in most countries. In each country I checked the legal age with a lawyer—not a camera buff or the local constable. The youngest model I photographed overseas was my Liechtenstein model. Naturally, I obtained (through the chaperon) written consent from her parents before setting up the session.

In golden-orange light, the next morning we began taking pictures on the grounds of the artist's home. Rarely have I had as charming and flexible a model. As quietly uninhibited as a kitten, she was in total rapport with her surroundings. Because she had posed for sketches, perhaps, she had far more patience than the average photographic model. Slowly, with almost feline grace, she moved from one locale to another. Distant foothills of the Alps, buildings, vegetation, walls, and lawns provided infinite variations in textures, backgrounds, and contrasts.

It is frequently hard for me to choose a single favorite picture in a set because so many locales bring back memories of an incident, a wisp of conversation, or an emotional highlight. In Liechtenstein I tried a photographic experiment that produced a special effect I like very much.

In order to obtain the ghost images of trees and clouds, first I photographed the trees and clouds with one-half the normal (meter reading) exposure for my medium-speed film. Next, without advancing the film, I had my 17-year-old model pose in an area of vegetation and photographed her with a normal exposure, also calculated by meter reading.

I don't consider this the esoteric ultimate that can be obtained by blending skies, vegetation, landscapes, or architecture with a nude through multiple exposures. In fact, it is for me just a beginning. The possibilities are so exciting that I have promised myself I will someday explore outdoor multiple exposure techniques in detail—using color film with colored filters as well as various black-and-white emulsions. With luck, I might even be able to photograph the same model in the same surroundings, in the fairyland principality of Liechtenstein.

Sweden

"Skal!" is the word they use in Sweden. It's pronounced "scawl" and, for me, it packs a two-way wallop. At a party (or other drinking occasion) you toast your host, hostess, their government, your government, the weather, the rutabaga crop, or anything handy with *"Skal!"* You say *"Skal"* as frequently as your thirst, or the parched condition of a companion's throat, dictates. If this first-aid treatment is rendered in the form of *snaps,* you can quickly become as marinated as a herring. That accounts for the first wallop.

The second wallop, for me, stems from the imbibing ceremony itself. You raise your glass, tip your head slightly, smile, and look deeply into your drinking partner's eyes. This crazy interlocking of gazes remains for the duration of your drink—truly, a charming, friendly custom. Or so I thought until I discovered that the eye contact was a traditional holdover from medieval times. It wasn't a Swede who disillusioned me. It was a foreigner like myself—a visitor from central Europe. With gimlet ice-flecks for eyes, he had a livid scar that ran from a notch in his right ear to the corner of his bristling white moustache. "In the days of chivalry, Mr. Rothman," he told me, "it was prudent to watch the eyes of every knight and wench with whom you drank. Otherwise, the liquor staining your vestments one day might be spilling out of your own slit gullet. *Skal!"*

In searching for a model, I wandered over most of the dozen islands on which Stockholm is built. There were the sunlit beaches dotting Saltsjon Bay, the vast stretches of greenery of Djurgarden Park, the majestic escarpments of the Town Hall with its three golden

Seemingly oblivious to the falling rain and her harsh surroundings, the model relaxes in a window and adjusts her hair; both shot at 1/60 sec. at *f*/11, Hasselblad 500C, 80mm lens.

crowns, and the area of Storyrkan with its priceless statues of Saint George and the Dragon. Everywhere I went, I found the Swedes cordially tolerant. They neither smiled at my walrus moustache nor flinched at the sounds of my clicking shutters. A toothy young man in an art supply shop located a model who suited me. She may have been his wife, sweetheart, landlord, or a village schoolteacher. I didn't ask. In Europe I found that too much curiosity doesn't pay. If people want you to know something, they'll tell you.

When time permits, I like to study a shooting locale in advance. The spot I chose in Sweden was a wooded finger of land that ended in a cliff pointing out to sea. In some ways it stirred memories of Diamond Head in Hawaii. For the better part of a day, I scouted the terrain, noting where shafts of sunlight struck craggy upheavals of rock that would provide contrasting backgrounds for human flesh, or tree-rimmed cover where dappled sunlight would enhance rounded femininity with gentler contrasts. My notes on exposure data, camera angles, and focal length lenses to be used were scribbled on the backs of my airline ticket envelope. In late afternoon I returned to my hotel with the satisfied feeling that everything was set for shooting the next day. With luck the land of the "*Skal*" should yield some of the best figure studies in my collection.

It was about midnight when the wind suddenly veered, and raindrops the size of pingpong balls began to splat against the windowpanes. By the time I slammed the windows shut, the drops had diminished to pea-size and were coming down so hard that the neon signs on the streets seemed to melt into out-of-focus wavers of color. By dawn it was drizzling steadily from a leaden sky. The mere thought of posing a model in the sodden woods gave me the chills. Too late, I realized that a more experienced photographer would have anticipated bad weather and located an alternate indoor locale. By ignoring the fickleness of weather, I was up the proverbial creek without a paddle.

As prearranged, however, the model and her chaperon joined me for early breakfast. Both were clearly apprehensive of cancellation. "It is too bad a day, yes?" the model asked.

"We'll find a place that's dry," I told her with more optimism than I felt. An idea popped into my mind. "We'll drive along the

The softness of the model is accentuated by the coarse brick wall; 1/60 sec. at *f*/8, Hasselblad 500C, 80mm lens.

Framed in the doorway of an old abandoned farmhouse with rain streaming down outside, the graceful, flowing body of the model contrasts strikingly with the stark reality of the old building; both shot at 1/60 sec. at *f*/8, Hasselblad 500C, 80mm lens.

coast and look for an abandoned building—a warehouse or fisherman's hut or even an old shipwreck."

"I know where there's a deserted farmhouse and barn," the chaperon said. "It's a long drive but . . . ."

I was already gathering my gear. "Let's go!"

The abandoned farmhouse with its variety of textured backgrounds, doorways, and roofless enclosures more than fulfilled my hopes. In addition to secluded shelter, the weathered aspect provided an atmosphere in perfect harmony with the gray bleakness of the day.

I've read about photographers who use conversation as a tool in evoking the moods and poses they want. I've also read about the opposite approach—the silent photographers who seldom speak to or direct a model. I don't fit neatly into either category. Sometimes I keep up a running fire of conversation, directing the model from one potential position to another. Again, I may simply follow as she moves about the set and speak only when I want her to hold a pose. As I see it, everything depends upon the temperament of the individual model, the circumstances, the moods of the moment, and the intent of your pictures.

With my Swedish model there was little need for talk. Tall, blonde, Junoesque, she was at perfect ease as she moved slowly and gracefully from one room to another. Instinctively, she seemed to sense when to pause and await the click of the shutter. Watching her in the viewfinder, I fancied she had a chameleon-like sensitivity to her immediate surroundings. In the presence of growing plants, her spirits seemed to soar, her face lighted, and her poses became animated. In the somber, rubble-strewn interior of the house, the contours of her body seemed to reflect a downcast, pensive mood.

The rain fell steadily as I exposed roll after roll of film. It was the chaperon who finally reminded me that the model was growing chilled and it was time to end the session. Reluctantly, I loaded my equipment into the rented car. Back in Stockholm the moment arrived for me once more to take leave of another model and chaperon whom I would never see again. This time there was a tradition to be observed. With each in turn, I bowed my head slightly in deference, smiled, and linked gazes over the rims of raised glasses, *"Skal!"*

A sculpture in the Millesgarten in Stockholm; 1/125 sec. at *f*/12.5, Hasselblad 500C, 150mm lens.

Heroic scale sculptures in the park at Oslo; 1/125 sec. at *f*/16, Hasselblad 500C, 80mm lens.

Norway

In Norway I spent hours photographing magnificent works of art, particularly the colossal statues of nudes around the Pillar of Life. Being an Alaskan, the Norwegian midnight sun was no novelty to me, nor was I intrigued with the tourist trips most Americans go in for. The prospect of a steamer trip into the fjords or an arctic safari into the polar bear and arctic seal country around *"Svalbard"* (Spitzenberg Island) literally left me cold. My time was limited, and I erred in spending so much of it on statues. When I got around to looking for a Norwegian model willing to pose out of doors, my allotted time ran out. This experience left two lessons indelibly printed in my mind.

First, it's a mistake to assume that your appearance, equipment, and a few tattered character references will convince people that your motives in photographing nudes are purely impersonal and artistic by nature. There were times I'd have given my best auxiliary lens for a few sample 11″ x 14″ enlargements and a half-dozen signed references from models who had posed for me in the United States. In Norway I made a bad mistake in being unable to show prospective nonprofessional subjects the kind of pictures I wanted to take.

The second lesson was this. You can't rely upon a model agency in most countries, especially the small or thinly populated ones, to provide a suitable subject for nude studies on short notice. If they turn up anyone at all, she's likely to be a showgirl, a part-time streetwalker, or a *femme fatale* with dollar signs for eyes. The professional cheesecake models that an agency sometimes provides are generally harder to work with than inexperienced subjects. They've been con-

Also in the park at Oslo; 1/125 sec. at *f*/11, Hasselblad 500C, 80mm lens.

ditioned to think in terms of their most successful cheesecake poses of the past. No matter how carefully you direct them away from cheesecake postures, they instinctively revert to what they consider a better stance the minute your back is turned. Moreover, they fail to realize that many cheesecake poses are too personal and provocative to be in good taste for nudes. My most unrewarding shooting sessions with nudes have been with professional cheesecake and "glamour" models. In Norway I didn't—couldn't—get a model of any type.

Denmark

In Denmark it was a different story. Whether it's my imagination or a provable fact I don't know, but the Danes seem to like Americans and I, for one, like the Danes. They seemed to see nothing unusual about a walrus-moustached American coming into Copenhagen with a load of cameras and announcing his intention of photographing Danish nudes on location. In fact, an old lady, who smoked a long black cigar (this being quite acceptable for little old ladies in Denmark), vowed she would pose for me herself if I had any trouble at all locating a "youngster under 50." As it was, I had no difficulty at all. A word dropped here and there turned up leads that, in turn, resulted in my choosing a blonde who seemed to me to epitomize Danish women.

As I've said before, I rarely ask a prospective model any more questions than absolutely necessary. The more questions you ask, the more she is challenged to reveal information about her personal life that has nothing to do with posing in the nude. Whenever possible, therefore, I had the chaperon check out the necessary details about a prospective model's age, the shooting schedule, hourly or by-day fees, and model releases. After a shooting session, it was the chaperon's job to pay the model and to tie up any other loose ends that might remain.

The locale I had selected in Denmark was a public beach about 30 miles northeast of Copenhagen. To obtain privacy as well as to take advantage of the early morning light, which I prefer above all other daylight, we left the city shortly after six A.M. Before seven o'clock we had found a long stretch of sandy beach bordered with

(Above) Model dipping her toe into the early morning surf; partially backlit; 1/125 sec. at *f*/12.5, Hasselblad 500C, 80mm lens.

(Opposite) The model is sitting amidst the tall grass resting for a moment between poses; 1/125 sec. at *f*/12.5, Hasselblad 500C, 80mm lens.

This pose was inspired by the statue of the Little Mermaid in the Copenhagen harbor; 1/125 sec. at *f*/12.5, Hasselblad 500C, 80mm lens, Plus-X film.

Model walking out into the early morning surf; backlit by the sun; 1/125 sec. at *f*/16, Hasselblad 500C, 80mm lens, Plus-X film.

patches of salt grass. The zooming, wheeling, squawking sea birds were the only other living creatures in sight.

As usual, I confined my directions to pointing out the places I wanted the model to pose—the shallow water, the beach itself, a clump of waving grass. Once she occupied that spot, I became as unobtrusive as possible, while waiting for the warmth of the rising sun, the mood of the sea, and her own thoughts to put her as nearly at natural ease as the circumstances permitted.

As the sun rose higher above the horizon, I moved from one spot to another, slowly circling my subject as I clicked away. To me, film has always been expendable, and even more so when I have a once-only opportunity to photograph a beautiful model thousands of miles away from Alaska. I had exposed over a dozen rolls of black-and-white and Ektacolor film before I noticed that the chaperon, out of camera range, was huddled in a blanket. This struck me as odd because neither the model nor I seemed to be uncomfortable. Not until I finished the 17th roll of film and said, *"Fini,"* did I realize that my shoes squished water with every step and the legs of my pants were wet up to my knees. Then, as if pierced by the cold for the first time, my model's teeth began to chatter. Without a word she dashed for the car and her clothes.

Back in Copenhagen, in dry clothes, I joined the chaperon and model for a late brunch. Viewing the model through the steam from our coffee cups, I found myself thinking how lovely she looked in clothing. It would be interesting, I supposed, if one had the time, to photograph her fully clothed. Then, my thoughts turned to the way she had looked with morning sunlight caressing the fresh, flowing contours of her body. The thought of 17 rolls of film waiting to be developed gave my spirits a spontaneous lift. I ordered a round of Benedictine and raised my glass to both model and chaperon, *"Skal!"*

Austria

There's a lot to be said for the cars built in Europe. I forget what make it was, but the car I rented in Vienna was a honey. The higher we climbed up the rolling, timbered shoulders of the Austrian Alps, the sweeter the four-cylinder motor of the compact seemed to purr.

It was comfortably warm inside the car, but when I rolled down the window to toss out a dead cigar butt, a blast of frigid air reminded me of our altitude. I glanced at my youthful model, Inga, wondering if the icy prelude had given her trepidations about posing in the nude. She was the quiet, pensive type who rarely spoke. Now, she was looking out the window and across the roof tops of the toy village to where a chalet perched like a cliff swallow's nest on the opposite mountain. Her thoughts were obviously drifting eons away from such mundane things as Alpine snowbanks. I glanced into the rearview mirror. Our middle-aged chaperon appeared to have fallen asleep in the back seat. I turned down the volume of the car radio. As I had suspected, she was snoring like a foghorn. I flipped up the volume, switched to a station playing Strauss' waltzes, and lit a fresh cigar. Blowing a cloud of pale blue smoke against the windshield, I decided that this was going to be another in an unbroken chain of perfect days in Austria.

Few countries in Europe appeal to me as much as Austria. Once a vast and mighty empire created by Charlemagne and ruled by a succession of Hapsburgs, the Republik Osterreich has been reduced by wars and intrigues to an area of about the size of the state of

High above Innsbruck from Mt. Hafelekar; 1/125 sec. at *f*/11, K2 filter, Hasselblad 500C, 80mm lens.

South Carolina. Yet, from the famous Blue Danube in the Vienna Basin to the snow-capped Tyrolean Alps, Austria literally seems to pulsate with a kaleidoscopic blending of beauty and culture. I was fascinated with the baroque architecture of the Mirabell Palace in Salzburg and the Belvedere Palace in Vienna, and with the formal gardens, the mirror-like lakes, the statues and paintings, and the music everywhere.

Most Austrians are a mixture of various nationalities—Czechs, Croats, Serbians, Slovenes, Slovaks, Italians, and Magyars. Everywhere I went, I found them to be a friendly and sociable people. Whether a musician from Vienna, a university student at Graz, or a vintner from beautiful Grinzing, the average Austrian impressed me as having, by American standards, a better than average understanding of creative works of art.

Deciding which type of figure, complexion, and hair color would best typify the Austrian woman as I saw her wasn't easy. Once I had a mental composite of her in my mind, it was a simple matter of describing my needs to friends in the comfortable atmosphere of *gemutlichkeit* in one of the traditional Viennese coffee houses. The very first model, Inga, who asked to come for an interview turned out to be the one I hired!

Now, high in the Alps above Innsbruck, I turned off the main road and followed a wooded trail that threaded across small shallow glens in which trickles of melted snow nourished blankets of wild ferns. I had forgotten the sleeping chaperon until I hit a pothole. As the car lurched, there was a thud followed by an explosive "*Ja!*" from the back seat. In the rearview mirror I glimpsed the chaperon's black straw hat canted at a rakish angle above her round startled face. Something told me she had whacked her head and was barely suppressing a comment about my driving, but at that point, the trees parted to the left and right. Dead ahead, although miles across a deep, thickly populated valley, loomed Hafelekar Mountain, my backdrop.

"We're here!" I said cheerily.

"*Ja,*" the chaperon said sourly.

My model said nothing. As I swung the car over to a level spot and stopped beside a stand of pines, I hoped that her quietness didn't portend inhibitions or an aversion to posing in the nude. If it did, I would be in for difficult, maybe fruitless, shooting. I like modesty in my models and insist that they disrobe in strict privacy and, between poses, wear a robe or blanket. A girl who is embarrassed or

An incredible fantasy-land park, illuminated by underground searchlights, in the center of Innsbruck where I went with my model night after night, but too many people prevented nude photography; 30 sec. at *f*/11, Hasselblad 500C, 80mm lens.

inhibited shouldn't pose at all. At best, her poses will be wooden portrayals of her self-conscious discomfort.

I need have had no fear about Inga. She and the chaperon disappeared into a thicket, and by the time I had unpacked my cameras she was back—as nonchalantly nude as though in the privacy of her own boudoir. Here, sheltered by timbered ridges on three sides, the fresh mountain air felt almost balmy in the sun. For the first time I saw Inga smile and, following the direction of her eyes, caught the chaperon yawning prodigiously. Although seemingly childlike and naïve in some ways, Inga apparently had a sense of humor as well as a beautiful body. I tilted my head toward the chaperon, winked, and grinned broadly at Inga. By now her smile was gone, but as she turned her gaze toward Hafelekar Mountain, I was sure I detected a twinkle in her eyes.

To say that we talked much during the shooting that morning would be gross exaggeration. We didn't talk at all. I had learned long before that you needn't speak a foreign language in order to direct a model to spots where you want them to pose or to refine the individual poses themselves. I had gradually adopted a series of sounds that were half grunts, half English words. "Uh-h-h-h, UH, Yes!" These, coupled with gestures, shrugs, and facial expressions worked magic to convey my wishes. Looking back on it now, I'm surprised that some of the girls didn't burst into laughter, or that a distant observer—and we knew they were occasionally around, although not always visible—didn't hail the police on the assumption that I was having some sort of seizure. Since I'm bearded and inclined to be a trifle portly, I must have looked odd when I stood on a high rock, with my rump pointed skyward as I bent forward from the hips, to direct a model on the ground below. With cameras dangling around my neck, flapping arms spread to direct a pose, and emitting "uh's and ah's," I must have looked like a gooney bird trying to take off and fly.

It wasn't until much later that I realized that Inga's gaze was directed downward in nearly every pose. This was an oversight on my part—a mistake. The visual effect in a picture suggests that her spirits were downcast. This wasn't the case at all. On the contrary, she was extremely interested in her immediate surroundings—the lichens on the ageless rocks, the mountain plants and mosses, and the ants and all other crawling, flying creeping denizens of this high altitude world. Again and again I clicked the shutter as she curiously examined the flora and fauna about her as if almost unaware of me or

(Above) Playing in the snow in the Austrian Alps; 1/125 sec. at *f*/11, Hasselblad 500C, 80mm lens.

(Opposite) Model framed by the tall pines with the Austrian Alps in the background; 1/125 sec. at *f*/11, Hasselblad 500C, 80mm lens.

(Above) Model relaxing in contemplation against an old rail fence; 1/125 sec. at *f*/11, Hasselblad 500C, 80mm lens.

(Opposite) Model resting for a moment between poses; 1/125 sec. at *f*/11, Hasselblad 500C, 150mm lens.

(Above) Playing in the snow in the Austrian Alps; 1/125 sec. at *f*/11, Hasselblad 500C, 150mm lens.

(Opposite) Fern shadows; 1/125 sec. at *f*/8, Hasselblad 500C, 150mm lens.

the camera. It was her naturalness and her complete rapport with her surroundings that began to interest me more than directed "poses." Hence, it wasn't until weeks later, when I studied contact proofs, that I noticed flaws in posture, unfortunate highlights, and other photographic shortcomings.

Even so, I am satisfied—as much so as I ever am with the results of a shooting session—with the pictures I took of Inga in the Austrian Alps. My favorite pictures, I think, are those that were taken in two locales within a few hundred feet of each other. In one spot, Inga knelt and reclined among lacy ferns that grew nearly as high as her shoulders. Here, the brilliant morning sunlight cast the shadows of the ferns over her arms and breasts in pleasingly patterned contrasts of black-and-white.

My other favorites are pictures taken on a partially sheltered tongue of late summer snow. Unmindful of the cold, Inga walked out upon the granulated snow and crouched to examine the debris that gusts of Alpine wind had deposited upon it. I shot several rolls of film in both black-and-white and color before she grew weary of the snow and moved slowly back in the direction of the car. As she paused from time to time, I finished up the film in my cameras. Clearly, she was growing tired and so was I.

As we drew near the car, we heard a rhythmic sound that reminded me of the distant rasp of a circular saw biting into an Alaskan pine. Together, we peeked into the car. The chaperon was sprawled diagonally across the back seat compartment, her hands comfortably folded across her plump middle, her mouth open, and her black hat riding up and down her forehead with each stentorian snore.

As Inga picked up her clothing and prepared to retire to the thicket to dress, our glances met for 1/1000 second. I'll never be sure, but I think she nearly smiled.

Darkroom Special Effects

I enjoy darkroom work almost as much as I enjoy shooting pictures. It's in the darkroom that one gets a second chance to exercise originality and creativity. By using techniques that are almost as old as photography itself, you can still come up with results as fresh—and sometimes as unpredictable—as tomorrow.

Access to a good enlarger is all you need to unleash more opportunities for image experimentation than you can test in a lifetime. In the portfolio pages that follow, some of the visual effects were obtained with the camera alone. Others are the result of off-beat printing techniques applied to normally exposed and developed negatives. A few represent the union of camera and enlarger manipulations. These are the techniques I use most often when something about a negative suggests experimenting for a "special effect." Texture screens yield a variety of distinctive patterns in photographic prints and are available through your photo store dealer in several popular sizes including 8″ x 10″ and 11″ x 14″. In appearance they resemble oversized negatives and should be treated as such by handling them only along the edges. Each texture screen has a definite pattern that will be reproduced on contact or enlarging paper, as will whatever scratches or fingerprints you accidentally add to the screen. In making an enlargement, the negative is focused upon the easel

This normal shot was combined in the enlarger with a small piece of a plastic tablecloth; 1/60 sec. at *f*/11, 4″ x 5″ Sinar View, 150mm lens.

in the usual way. With a sheet of enlarging paper on the easel, the texture screen is simply placed directly in contact with it, sandwiched between the emulsion (dull) sides of the negative and the texture screen. The exposure time required for the enlargement (or for making textured contact prints if you prefer) will be approximately one and one-half to two times normal.

There are at least half a dozen relatively inexpensive commercial texture screens to choose from. I frequently use a "dry point etching" screen that produces a pattern of interlacing fine lines over the entire print after the manner of an artist's etching. I also like a "tapestry" screen that gives a print the appearance of having been reproduced on coarse woven material such as monk's cloth or canvas. (Other tapestry screens are available, if you want the visual effect of a print reproduced on finely woven tapestry material.) If texture screen printing interests you, I suggest that you also examine the patterns of "bromoil," "paper negative," and "steel-line."

Sandwiching negatives in the negative carrier of the enlarger is sometimes easier explained than performed. In theory, you simply combine two or more negatives in the carrier—say an overall negative of clouds and a shot of a nude—so they can be projected and printed simultaneously. Occasionally, you find two negatives so compatible that they can be easily printed as a "sandwich," but most "sandwich" combinations require considerable dodging or printing in of scattered areas during enlargement.

A variation on the negative-sandwiching technique is that of combining a negative with other materials in the enlarger carrier. I've tried crinkled and colored cellophane, thin sheets of textured and patterned glass, reticulated negative patterns, and various other partially translucent materials such as plastics. I've also experimented with dyes, paints, and opaque substances daubed, sprayed, or spatter-painted on sheets of clear glass or film which, in turn, were sandwiched in the enlarger carrier with a negative to be projected. One thing I don't recommend is tampering with a prize negative before you have experimented with a series of reject negatives. One of my friends, who doctored some of his best negatives with concoctions ranging from mineral oil and new coccine to sugar paste and acetone, learned the cost of experimentation the hard way.

To me, double or multiple printing, reticulation, the making of patterned montages, solarizations, and dozens of other special techniques are fair game in the darkroom. Many of the older photographic hobby publications such as *Minicam Photography*, *Camera*,

(Above) This study in repose is faintly reminiscent of the style of the Old Masters. Techdata, 1/60 sec. at *f*/8, 4″ x 5″ Sinar View, 150mm lens.

This photograph, which resembles a line drawing, was made by first shooting a normal negative with contrasty lighting. The negative was contact printed onto a piece of litho film producing a litho positive, which was contact printed onto another piece of litho film. After unwanted detail was opaqued out, the remainder was printed onto another piece of litho film. This final negative was used to make the prints; 1/60 sec. at *f*/8, 4″ x 5″ Sinar View, 150mm lens.

and *American Photography* printed definitive articles on darkroom legerdemain. Now that most hobby magazines have placed their emphasis upon new products and/or color experimentation, the hobbyist interested in black-and-white darkroom experiments will have to haunt the reference libraries for how-to-do-it details. One technique I would like to touch upon briefly is my favorite variation on bas-relief printing. (Some people refer to it as "drop-out relief printing.")

The end result sometimes yields an optical illusion of three-dimensional depth. At other times, only a few stark lines delineate the contours of a nude, the details having been completely "dropped out" during the processing of a series of copy negatives from a single original negative. Everything depends upon the way in which the negatives are handled, *i.e.*, how many times they are repeatedly contact printed to produce near-duplicate positive and negative transparencies, and how the final positive/negative transparencies are sandwiched together for printing. Here is the basic method I use in making most of the bas-relief (or drop-out relief) prints in this portfolio.

Simplicity is the key to dramatic results. Your subject should be posed in simple, uncluttered surroundings. The fewer and plainer the props, the better. A solid black or dark-colored roll of paper that provides an unbroken or seamless background and floor area is ideal.

The pose should be kept simple, because strong contours in the lines of the body are essential. Essential, too, is strong, contrasty lighting. Side or rimlighting generally produces the most dramatic effects.

First, make a negative with a normal exposure.

Second, contact print the original negative onto another piece of film. I prefer litho film for the copying process, but it is possible to use other types of emulsion—the contrastier the better. When developed, the second piece of film will yield a positive image—actually, a black-and-white transparency.

Third, contact print the positive on still another piece of film to obtain a negative once-removed from your original negative. (You may as well put the original negative on file at this point, because the actual prints will eventually be made from dupes.) The negative you have just contact printed from the positive will have begun to lose some of its gray scale. That's what you are seeking—the dropping out of gray scale details.

"The Dream." One photograph was taken of the two frames hung by wire against a black background, with a branch and two stuffed birds in one frame, and several mouthfuls of cigar smoke. The other negative was of the model with normal lighting behind a piece of lace. The model was exposed at 1/60 sec. at *f*/8, Hasselblad 500C, 80mm lens; the frames were exposed at 1/30 sec. at *f*/8, Hasselblad 500C, 50mm lens.

The more times you alternate back and forth to produce a new positive from the last negative and *vice versa,* the fewer details and the less gray scale that will remain.

Let's say, though, that you stop making contact negatives and positives after step three and decide to try your first print on paper.

All you have to do is sandwich the duplicate negative and positive together so that they are slightly offset (out-of-register in the contour lines) and make a contact print in the usual way. If necessary, trim the negative slightly to fit into the contact printer or enlarger carrier.

If you are satisfied with the results you obtain at this point, well and good. As I said, since I enjoy darkroom work more than some photographers do, I generally go a step or two further. With the positive and negative dupes sandwiched together out-of-register, I frequently make still another contact-printed negative with material having a built-in dot pattern. (As an alternate experiment, you might try making a contact-printed negative of the sandwiched dupes, together with one of the texture screens mentioned above.)

As a final step, I use liquid opaquing material to eliminate unwanted detail remaining on the dupes. After the opaque is thoroughly dry, I make a final contact print on film, which becomes my master negative.